BAL

Richard Nelson

BROADWAY PLAY PUBLISHING INC
New York
www.broadwayplaypublishing.com
info@broadwayplaypublishing.com

BAL

© Copyright 1998 by Richard Nelson

First published by B P P I in December 1998 in *Plays By Richard Nelson, Early Plays Volume Two*
This edition: December 2016

I S B N: 978-0-88145-753-7

Book design: Marie Donovan
Page make-up: Adobe InDesign
Typeface: Palatino

BAL was first presented by The Williamstown Second Company in the summer of 1979, directed by Martin Kapell.

BAL was produced subsequently by The Goodman Theater (Gregory Mosner, Artistic Director) on 6 March 1980. The cast and creative contributors were:

BAL...Jim Belushi
JOHNNY..Cosmo White
SOPHIE ....Caitlin Clarke
JOHANNA...Lora Staley
DUSZAK ....Del Close
EMILY DUSZAK/FEMALE SINGER ....Patricia Hodges
PLANTER/CRAP-PLAYER..............................Michael Saad
ZEIGLER/PRIEST/CRONY ....John E Mohrlein
YOUNG WOMAN .... Ellen Crawford
MAN/MAN WITH FISHING POLE........... Dennis Kennedy
YOUNG MAN... Leland Crooke
MAN WHO ACTS LIKE BEAST/WAITER..... Daniel Cooney
MAN WHO ACTS LIKE BEAST/BOSS .... Ron Dean
GUEST ....Belinda Bremner

Director.. Gregory Mosher
Costumes..Dunya Ramicova
Lights ....Jennifer Tipton

CHARACTERS

Bal
Johnny
Duszak
Emily Duszak
Zeigler
Planter
Young Man
Young Woman
Man
Johanna
Two Men Who Acts Like Beasts
Crap-Player
Man With Fishing Pole
Priest
Sophie
Boss
Crony
Female Singer
Waiter

BAL is for Marty Kapell and Jennifer Tipton

Scene One (a)

(A field. Night. BAL *[thirties] and* JOHNNY *[early twenties] lie on their backs looking at the stars.* JOHNNY *has a notepad. Music in the distance. Pause)*

JOHNNY: I took your advice and talked to Johanna. *(No response)* My girl?

BAL: Oh. And…?

JOHNNY: And nothing. We talked. Or rather she did. She claims it has nothing to do with me, and if she were to go to bed with anyone, it would certainly be with me. But right now, she has a lot of things to figure out about herself. She says, she wants to know who she is before getting too involved in anything…. I don't know. I can wait, if that's what she wants; that is, if I have to. But, Jesus Christ, I don't know. What do you think, Bal? She's only sixteen.

BAL: What do I think?

*(*JOHNNY *nods.)*

BAL: I think many things, Johnny. One moment this. The next something else. Some of my thoughts are pretty stupid. Some are fantastic. Some have changed my life. Others have bored me to tears. I think a lot of things. Bal does. *(Short pause—looks back at the stars)* Is it wrong to want to feel?

JOHNNY: *(Opening up his notepad, set to write)* Go ahead, Bal, I'm listening.

BAL: *(Continuing his thought)* I mean, in a certain way, I wish we didn't know what we know, or maybe that what we knew we found out was wrong. How I would love to look up at the stars and the moon and say— "what fools we were to think that we were spinning; to think that we were on an earth which revolves." I would love to pity the poor scientists. I would love to once again believe that we were at the center of things, that all moved around us. Then I wouldn't feel like I was missing something. Then I wouldn't be bothered by not being able to feel us moving. If we are spinning, is it really wrong to want to feel it? And if I can't feel it, I'd rather not know we were moving at all.

JOHNNY: Beautiful, Bal.

BAL: *(Getting up)* That's enough of that for tonight.

JOHNNY: I can hardly wait to finish this profile. The notes I've already submitted, you can't imagine what a stir they've created. My editor's even talking about a cover, Bal.

BAL: Listen.

(We hear the music in the distance.)

BAL: That party won't last forever. Come on, I need a drink. *(He starts to go.)* I want to feel myself spinning.

Scene One (b)

(DUSZAK's dining room. Music. Food. Drink. DUSZAK, a wealthy businessman; EMILY DUSZAK, his attractive wife; ZIEGLER, an employee; PLANTER, a servant; YOUNG MAN; YOUNG WOMAN; and MAN [guests]. Also BAL and JOHNNY, who sits at a table and eats.)

DUSZAK: Planter, another bottle of Bordeaux!

PLANTER: Yes, Mister Duszak. *(Hurries out)*

DUSZAK: I can tell, Ziegler, that you think Old Duszak's being a bit extravagant.

ZIEGLER: I wasn't thinking anything of the kind, sir. Though there are but four or five bottles of Bordeaux left in the cellar.

DUSZAK: I know perfectly well what is and what is not in my own cellar, Ziegler. So there are only four or five bottles of Bordeaux left. The question is, Ziegler, *why* are they left?

ZIEGLER: Why, sir?

DUSZAK: Because I have been hoarding them. And why have I been hoarding them, Ziegler?

ZIEGLER: Why, sir?

DUSZAK: For a reason, that's why. And what sort of reason am I suggesting, Ziegler?

ZIEGLER: What, sir?

DUSZAK: For a *very good* reason, that's what. Ziegler, man has reasons for what he does. He has a mind. He thinks. He reasons. I am a man. I have a mind, I think. So I have my reasons!

ZIEGLER: I'm sure you must, sir.

DUSZAK: *And* if I have my reasons for hoarding my Bordeaux, then it is fair to assume that I have my reasons for uncorking it as well. Ziegler, man thinks. Man has new thoughts. Man changes his mind. And man finds new reasons! And what sort of reasons must a man find to change his mind?

ZIEGLER: I give up, sir.

DUSZAK: Very good reasons, that's what!!

ZIEGLER: Makes sense, sir.

DUSZAK: And what could be a better reason than…
(Waves his arms, pointing out the room)

ZIEGLER: Than what, Sir?

DUSZAK: *(Yelling)* Mister Bal!!!

EVERYONE: *(Stopping their chitchat and toasts)* To Mister Bal!!!

BAL: Pass the sausage plate, please. *(He eats.)*

YOUNG WOMAN: *(Slightly drunk)* Mister Duszak, would you tell us again how you found our guest of honor?

MAN: *(To* YOUNG MAN*)* I love this story, don't you?

*(*YOUNG MAN *and* MAN *go back into conversation.)*

DUSZAK: You can't want to hear it *again!*

(Everyone is back to their chitchat, no response. Short pause)

DUSZAK: But if I must, I must.

EMILY: *(Passing out sausages)* Go ahead, dear. You speak so well.

DUSZAK: Well, I know when my arm is being twisted. Man resists. But man overcomes his resistance. And man grows! So, to begin at the beginning, it was Johnny here who first brought Mister Bal to my attention. Johnny.

JOHNNY: *(Taking a sausage from* EMILY*)* Well, my generator had gone on the whosits. I called the repair shop and Mister Bal was sent to fix it. He arrived late in the afternoon, around five or half past, and as I wrote that night in my journal, my first impression of him was one of, and I quote: "a man who remembers his dreams, a man who knows, and a man who lives."

*(*YOUNG MAN *applauds.)*

ZIEGLER: *(To* YOUNG MAN*)* Shut up, we're not finished with the story yet.

DUSZAK: *(To others, who only casually listen)* You notice how my secretary, Mister Ziegler, says "we" when he means me. How odd to express such participation when only a moment ago he was questioning whether Mister Bal was worthy of such a celebration.

EMILY: *(To* ZIEGLER*)* No!

ZIEGLER: I wasn't saying…

DUSZAK: Of course you weren't saying. You never say. You insinuate. That's all you ever do. That's your type, Ziegler. In this world there are those who insinuate and those who…

ZIEGLER: Who what?

DUSZAK: I forget. *(Grabs his glass)* To Mister Bal!

EVERYONE: *(Stopping their chitchat for a moment to toast)* Mister Bal!

BAL: Is there any mustard?

*(*PLANTER, *who has returned with the wine, runs out after mustard.)*

DUSZAK: But to continue with our story. Johnny here kept talking about this remarkable young mechanic he had met. In fact, you could say that every third word out of Johnny's mouth was "Bal."

JOHNNY: Bal this. Bal that.

DUSZAK: The "ideas" of Bal. The languages that this Bal knew. The books that this man, Bal, had read.

JOHNNY: I drove you crazy, Mister Duszak.

BAL: *(Eating)* But you couldn't help yourself.

DUSZAK: Johnny drove me crazy. But he kept saying he couldn't help himself.

*(*ZIEGLER, *a little drunk now, drops a glass, which shatters.)*

DUSZAK: Control yourself, Ziegler. *(Back to the story)* Last week I would have sworn I knew every single educated man left in our district. So you can imagine how incredulous I was. But still one never really knows, does one?

ZIEGLER: Never.

DUSZAK: Man is curious, he questions, he explores! So I felt it almost my duty to meet with this young mechanic, named Bal, and quiz him. And we subsequently met for the first time at Johnny's. And believe me when I say this, but I pulled no punches. I mean, bushes, in my opinion, were not made to be beaten around, if you catch my meaning. So I wanted to know right from the start whether I was wasting my time. So I said to Mister Bal, I said—

JOHNNY: "True hope is swift, and flies with swallow's wings; Kings it makes gods, and meaner creatures kings."

DUSZAK: And Mister Bal, without so much as a breath, replied—what did you reply, Mister Bal?

BAL: *(Reaching for more sausages, with his mouth full) Richard the Third,* Act Five, Scene Two.

DUSZAK: What more is there to say!! To Mister Bal!!

EVERYONE: *(Toasting)* Mister Bal!

(EMILY gives DUSZAK a kiss as others applaud the end of the story.)

JOHNNY: *(To BAL)* Are you enjoying yourself? You've been terribly quiet.

(BAL knocks over a glass.)

JOHNNY: You're not drinking too much, are you, Bal?

BAL: Man eats. Man drinks. Man vomits.

ZIEGLER: *(To a guest, holding his stomach)* Excuse me. *(Hurries out)*

BAL: Ziegler is a man.

DUSZAK: *(Pushing* JOHNNY *aside)* Excuse me, Johnny. Mister Bal, I just wanted to tell you—before you get the wrong idea, I just wanted to tell you that if it were only up to me, I would, of course, say: "Of course. A man of your talents deserves the top." I would say that, Mister Bal. And I would mean it, too. But it is not up to me.

BAL: *(Trying to stare at* EMILY*)* It's not up to you.

DUSZAK: That's correct. There are other employees, there's seniority, there'd be jealousy. But you're a man of the world, you know how these things work. They take time.

BAL: I know how things work.

DUSZAK: So I will come right to the point then. That's the sort of man I am, Mister Bal. You'll soon learn that working for me.

BAL: I'll learn.

DUSZAK: So here is what I have in mind. I'm thinking—why not bring Mister Bal in as a foreman. A foreman, Mister Bal, it's not the top, but it sure beats being a mechanic. Foreman, I am thinking—foreman…

BAL: And I'm thinking that you are blocking my view.

DUSZAK: What? Oh, of course. This is not the time to talk shop. *(Backs off)* We'll talk later. We'll talk. Don't worry, when I say we'll talk…

BAL: We'll talk.

*(*DUSZAK *moves away;* EMILY *comes by with a tray.)*

PLANTER: *(To* YOUNG WOMAN*)* My uncle once had a barber who spoke ancient Greek.

EMILY: *(To* BAL*)* You're very quiet. I hope we haven't put you off. *(He just stares at her.)* Johnny tells me you might be looking for a new apartment.

BAL: Who isn't?

EMILY: Do you really live in an attic, Mister Bal?

BAL: Is that what Johnny says? *(He drinks.)*

EMILY: He says there rats and awful smells from the street. And he says you never lock your door or close a window. Is that wise, Mister Bal, not to lock your door?

(No response; BAL stares.)

EMILY: Johnny says you love fresh air.

(BAL stares.)

EMILY: He says you've written books yourself, which you've burned. He says that you told him those books were written only for you.

(BAL stares.)

EMILY: He says, Mister Bal is the most fascinating person he has ever met.

(BAL holds his head, feeling a bit dizzy.)

EMILY: My husband owns a few buildings, and I'm sure you could get into one if you'd like…. See, I think about creature comforts. I think a person's surroundings are very important, don't you? …I'm scared of rats myself…. Maybe I should get you some coffee, Mister Bal.

BAL: I would like that. I enjoy watching you walk.

(EMILY leaves.)

YOUNG MAN: I'll ask him. I'm not afraid to ask him.

PLANTER: Then ask him. No one's stopping you.

YOUNG WOMAN: He is just a mechanic after all.

PLANTER: And he's just been sitting there.

YOUNG WOMAN: If you won't, then I will….

YOUNG MAN: No. I'll do it. I said I'll do it, so I will. *(Goes up to BAL)* Mister Bal…

(BAL *turns to him.*)

YOUNG MAN: Uh....

YOUNG WOMAN: Mister Bal, we were all wondering, since you have been so...quiet. You have been very, very quiet.

YOUNG MAN: Hardly said a word all night, Mister Bal.

YOUNG WOMAN: Hardly a...

PLANTER: And now that you've had the chance to get to know us...well, we'd sort of like to...

YOUNG MAN: We'd be very interested in...

YOUNG WOMAN: We want to get to know...

ALL THREE: You!

ZIEGLER: *(Who has just returned and heard this)* Speech! Speech!

EVERYONE: Speech! Speech!

(Commotion settles down. Pause. Everyone looks at BAL.)

BAL: You want to know what's on my mind? What I'm thinking?

(Everyone nods.)

BAL: I see. Just give me a second or two to collect myself.

(Pause, everyone waits, then finally—)

BAL: I'm thinking—sausages. Good sausages. I'm thinking I wonder when was the last time I had sausages like... But, you know, I can't remember when it was. I'm thinking how I can't remember. I'm thinking, how it must have been a long time ago. *(Short pause)* I'm thinking, on the whole, you are probably pretty decent people. Helpful. Nice. You know. I'm thinking on the other hand that you are also assholes. And I'm thinking I will most probably ridicule you

like crazy in the days to come. That sort of thing....
I'm thinking I can't eat another sausage. I'm feeling
bloated. I'm thinking how can I use you. A job. An
apartment. How can I take advantage. Something
along those lines.... What else? Uh, I'm thinking I
shouldn't have drunk as much as I have. I feel sort of
dizzy. I'm concerned about being sick to my stomach.
I'm afraid of embarrassing myself. I'm wondering if I
will be constipated in the morning.... I'm thinking—
am I speaking out of turn, saying all this? Will they
resent me? Then—will I care? And what else?

(EMILY *comes in with the coffee.*)

BAL: Oh yes. There is one more thing. The wife over
there. What's your name?

EMILY: *(Confused by the silence of the party)* Emily.

BAL: I am feeling this strong urge to get on top of her.
I am. I'm feeling that. And I'm also thinking that I will
try to keep her in mind, I will try to think of her, the
next time I masturbate.

(*Long silence as the lights fade.*)

Scene Two (a)

(*A rowdy bar. Tables. Noise.* JOHNNY, EMILY, *and*
JOHANNA *[*JOHNNY's *young girlfriend] sit at one table.*
EMILY *is crying,* JOHNNY *and* JOHANNA *are uncomfortable.
At another table,* BAL *is telling a funny story to the* TWO
MEN WHO ACT LIKE BEASTS. *They laugh wildly.*)

JOHANNA: Emily, are you okay?

(EMILY *nods, though keeps crying.*)

JOHANNA: *(To* JOHNNY*)* I just don't understand how
you could bring me to such a revolting place. I thought
I knew you, Johnny, but now I'm beginning to wonder.

JOHNNY: Bal thought we'd enjoy seeing something besides the ends of our own noses, Johanna. He thought we should see the hairs in our noses and the warts on the human face.

JOHANNA: How pretentious! This Mister Bal of yours is just a con man. He's making a fool out of you, Johnny.

JOHNNY: If that's what he's doing, then I'd rather be a fool than a snob. Admit it, maybe you're not enjoying yourself now, but in a day or two you'll be boasting like crazy about having seen all this.

JOHANNA: Five minutes more. That's all. Then I'm going home with or without you.

JOHNNY: Five minutes! Fine. Five minutes to teach you that there's a world beyond your turned-up nose!

(Laughter from BAL *and the* TWO MEN. BAL *wanders over to* EMILY; *he holds an almost empty bottle.)*

BAL: *(To* EMILY*)* Do you have any more cash? This bottle's about had it.

JOHNNY: *(Reaching into his pocket)* Bal, here's some....

*(*BAL *gestures for him to put away his money.* BAL *continues to stare at* EMILY.*)*

EMILY: What were you talking about with those men?

(Pause. BAL *takes her purse.)*

BAL: *(Finally)* You.

(Horse-laughter from the TWO MEN. EMILY *suddenly grabs her purse and hugs it.)*

JOHANNA: *(Standing)* I'm sorry, but I'm leaving....

EMILY: *(To* JOHANNA*)* Please, no!

*(*JOHANNA *stops.)*

BAL: *(To* EMILY*)* You seem to have almost a sexual attachment to that purse. *(To* JOHNNY*)* You know, I once had the same kind of thing with an old brown wallet. Kept patting it. Especially in crowds. Even when I had no money. So it wasn't just that I was patting it to feel secure. I think it was more because the wallet was soft leather. *(Turns back to* EMILY*)* I was telling those two men there what you are like. I mean, your positions; what you moaned. I also told them something else, what was it? Oh right, I remember. I told them how you taste. I let them smell my fingers...

*(*EMILY *cries.)*

JOHANNA: *(To* JOHNNY*)* Stop him!

JOHNNY: Bal...

BAL: Johnny, she asked. She did ask.

EMILY: *(Crying)* You're disgusting!

BAL: That doesn't tell me anything I don't already know. But on the other hand, I'm always fascinated by how other people see me. No matter what they say, that I'm cruel or terrific, doesn't much matter. What I like is that they are talking about me and giving me another point of view from which I can relate to me. That makes me feel in touch with myself.

*(*EMILY *bursts out crying; she tries to hit* BAL*, but he catches her blows. The* TWO MEN *come closer to watch.)*

JOHANNA: *(*JOHNNY *gestures to her for them to leave.)* We can't leave her!

BAL: *(To* EMILY*)* Now look what you've done—you've drawn a crowd. A man stands next to a woman who's sobbing. People will begin to draw conclusions, Emily. And it's the man who will be fingered as the guilty party. And once he begins to feel their hostile stares, he'll want to crawl away and hide. Emily, you've made me feel like I want to crawl away and hide. You have, Emily. *(Screams at her)* You!!!... You've made me feel guilty.

EMILY: I don't know what I ever saw in you!

JOHANNA: He's just sick!

BAL: *(To* JOHANNA*)* Mmmmmm. I too can make judgments of other people. For example, I find her boring. But the moment I make such a judgment, I find myself judging the judgment. Was it "boring" I really meant to say, or was it "tiresome"? That kind of thing.

EMILY: *(Breaks away from* BAL*)* This is a nightmare!

BAL: Now there you have another thing I find people always doing. I see them relating one experience to another—just as you did there with "nightmare" and our situation here—but I wonder if what in fact people really should be doing is trying to precisely articulate for themselves just one experience at a time. Do you see what I mean? But as I'm sure you noticed, I did the very same thing with your purse and my patting my wallet. So who am I to say?

EMILY: Stop him! What are you doing to me?!!!

BAL: What? You don't know? I'm abusing you, Emily. I am being very cruel, even vicious. I am being a bastard. All that is quite clear to me, isn't it to you? *(To* JOHNNY*)* She asked.

*(*EMILY*, crying, moves to leave. The* TWO MEN *suddenly grab her, and attempt to hug and kiss her. She fights and screams.* JOHANNA *screams.* JOHNNY *hesitates, first looking at* BAL*, then at the* TWO MEN*; then he tries to pull them off* EMILY*.* JOHANNA *helps. She picks up a small chair and tries to hit them.)*

JOHANNA: Get off her! Get the fuck off her!! Fuck you! Fuck you! Fuck you!

(Suddenly, the TWO MEN *stop and simply walk away.* EMILY *cries;* JOHANNA *hugs her;* JOHNNY *breathes heavily.)*

JOHNNY: Bal, why didn't you try to stop that?

BAL: *(Yells)* Because I started that!! Boy, are you thick. Emily's been hanging around my neck for a week, I'm sick of her…. I find that despicable of me, don't you?

JOHANNA: *(Hugging* EMILY*)* She's cut herself. You ought to be ashamed of yourself.

BAL: I am.

JOHANNA: Come. We'll wash it out.

JOHNNY: Bal, what's gotten into you?

BAL: *(Grabs* JOHANNA's *hand)* Your hands are shaking, are your legs shaking too?

(She pulls away.)

JOHNNY: *(To* JOHANNA*)* He's usually not like this.

EMILY: *(To* JOHANNA*)* He isn't.

JOHANNA: I'm sure.

JOHNNY: It's the whiskey.

JOHANNA: Yes.

EMILY: It is. It's the whiskey.

JOHANNA: Yes.

EMILY: You don't think I'd go with a man who *always* acted like that, do you?

*(*EMILY *and* JOHANNA *leave in the direction of the bathroom.)*

BAL: You're right. It is the whiskey…. And when it's not the whiskey, then it's my upbringing. And when it's not my upbringing, then it's my environment. When it's not my environment, then it's something else. My schooling maybe. Or how about my diet?… Do you have any cash, I want another bottle.

JOHNNY: Bal, I think you've had enough.

BAL: So do I. *(Calls)* Waiter! Another bottle!

Scene Two (b)

(Bathroom of the bar. JOHANNA *looks at the shoulder of* EMILY's *dress.)*

EMILY: It's ripped, isn't it? It's ruined.

JOHANNA: It's on the seam.

EMILY: It's ripped. He ripped it.

JOHANNA: It's on the seam.

EMILY: I'll never wear it again. I can't.

JOHANNA: Only if you don't want to.

EMILY: I don't. I can't *(Suddenly)* I'm drugged! That's how he got me here. Don't you see? He slipped something into a drink. Who'd have thought. I mean, who would ever have thought. You can't blame me, I'm drugged! *(Turns to* JOHANNA, *no response)* No. But I wish I were. I wish I were something. If not drugged then I wish I had a mental illness. I wish I were out of my senses…

JOHANNA: I have a safety pin in my pocketbook. *(She leaves.)*

EMILY: "I have a safety pin in my pocketbook." Go to hell. *(She tries to see the rip but can't. She takes off her dress, wears only a slip. Looks at the rip.)* It's on the seam.

*(*JOHANNA *returns with her pocketbook, starts to pin the dress.)*

EMILY: So I like sex, so shoot me.

JOHANNA: You don't have to explain.

EMILY: I don't, do I? That's a good one. I'll have to remember that. So I don't have to explain. Just who are you to say that to me?!!! *(She cries, covering her face with her dress. Pause)*

JOHANNA: Emily? *(No response)* Emily, look, I'll make a little confession of my own.

(EMILY looks up.)

JOHANNA: I'll bet that if I didn't watch my step, I too could find myself falling for this Mister Bal.

(EMILY looks at JOHANNA.)

JOHANNA: See, you shouldn't blame yourself. It could happen to anyone.

EMILY: You're lying, aren't you?

JOHANNA: No.

EMILY: You're just trying to make me feel better, aren't you?

(Pause)

JOHANNA: Yes.

EMILY: You're lying?

JOHANNA: Yes.

EMILY: Good. Bal wouldn't give you the time of day. I'd hate to see you disappointed.

Scene Two (c)

(The bathroom. EMILY, alone, putting on her makeup.)

EMILY: Bastard. Son of a bitch. Slime. Shit.

(JOHANNA enters.)

JOHANNA: Emily?

EMILY: I'm not upset.

JOHANNA: Johnny says if you want to, you could come out now.

EMILY: Nothing happened. Why should I be upset?

JOHANNA: We'll make sure you get home alright. Johnny and me.

EMILY: Rise—that's what I always do. That's how I was brought up. Rise above the stench, hold your nose and lift your head.

JOHANNA: Bal says he is sorry.

EMILY: For what? Nothing happened.

JOHANNA: He's been dancing. He's put on almost a show. He's very funny. Bal is.

EMILY: Rise. *(Stands up)*

JOHANNA: He even tried to get Johnny to get up and dance. But he'd have no part of that.

EMILY: I'm holding my nose. See. That's how I was brought up. *(Leaves)*

JOHANNA: *(After a pause, looks in the mirror)* Whoa. I haven't danced like this in ages. *(Fans herself; stops)* Even my legs are shaking.

Scene Two (d)

(Bathroom. EMILY and JOHANNA enter talking. Both out of breath from dancing.)

JOHANNA: I think I liked it best when we didn't know who we were supposed to be dancing with. Then I wasn't thinking so much. Then I wasn't trying to be so good at it. I could just sort of let go. *(She giggles.)*

EMILY: Then do. *(Takes off her shoes)* I shouldn't have worn these shoes.

JOHANNA: Do what?

EMILY: Let go. Abandon yourself. Feel the breeze on your cheeks. You're old enough. You told me yourself Johnny's almost begged you.

JOHANNA: He has, but I couldn't. I've thought too much about it. I want to wait until I'm done thinking about it.

EMILY: Flower, woman, flower!

JOHANNA: No.

EMILY: That means yes.

JOHANNA: Maybe.

EMILY: That really means yes. Johnny's not so bad. You'll like it. You'll love it.

JOHANNA: Maybe.

EMILY: You want some advice?

JOHANNA: No.

(EMILY *rubs her feet; dance music grows in the background.* JOHANNA *dances, stops.*)

EMILY: *(Looks up at* JOHANNA, *obviously thinking.)* So I like sex…

(JOHANNA *turns to* EMILY.)

JOHANNA: *(Innocently)* So shoot me.

(EMILY *and* JOHANNA *laugh.*)

Scene Two (e)

(Bathroom. JOHANNA *alone.)*

JOHANNA: *(To herself)* Mother, Father, close your eyes. And sleep well tonight. I'm grown up. And that can't be helped. *(Recites)*
"Although I joy in thee,
I have no joy of this contract to-night,
It is too rash, too unadvis'd, too sudden,
Too like the lightning, which doth cease to be
Ere one can say it lightens."

How I hated it when Mister Peters made the whole
class memorize that. *(Recites)*
"This bud of love, by summer's ripening breath,
May prove a beauteous flower when next we meet.
Good-night, good-night! as sweet repose and rest
Come to thy heart as that within thy breast!"
(Short pause) Thank you, Mister Peters. Thanks. *(Leaves, calling)* Johnny! Johnny!

Scene Three (a)

(BAL's attic. Bed. JOHANNA in bed, covering herself with the covers. He sits on the edge of the bed.)

JOHANNA: I don't believe what I've done. How did this happen?

BAL: First, I unbuttoned your blouse, then I stuck your hand inside my pants....

(JOHANNA covers her ears.)

BAL: You asked me a question.

JOHANNA: I'm confused. This room. I don't even know where I am.

BAL: You can start by blaming your sweetheart, Johnny. If that boy could hold his liquor, he wouldn't have passed out and left me to take you home.

JOHANNA: Then why didn't you?! Why didn't you just take me home?!!

BAL: It must have been the whiskey.

JOHANNA: They'll notice. Everyone will notice. I can't go back there. I can't. *(Quickly turns to BAL)* Bal, I love you. Let's go away, Bal. Dear, come. I'll write home. After we're settled, my parents can come and visit. They'll see I did the right thing. I'll show them. They'll

forgive and forget. Where's my blouse? *(Hysterical)*
Where's my blouse?!!!

(BAL *has been sitting on it. He hands it to* JOHANNA.)

JOHANNA: Well—pack! What are you waiting for?
Pack!!!!

BAL: The only place I'm going is into the bathroom. I
want to wash myself.

JOHANNA: What?!! You have to go with me! *(Short
pause)* I want that!!! *(She collapses; to herself.)* God, what
was I thinking of. Go away with…I'd sooner die. I'd
sooner slit my wrists. No one will know. I don't look
so different. Do I? Do I?!! And who's going to find out?
I'm not going to tell anybody. I'm not going to tell a
soul. And you won't either, will you? *(Short pause)* Will
you?!!!

BAL: I never know what I'm going to do. Only what
I've already done, Johanna.

JOHANNA: Promise me!!! *(No response)* Promise me!!!!!!

BAL: As a matter of fact, knowing me as I do, once I see
my best friend Johnny's face, I'm probably not going to
be able to resist telling. Just out of curiosity, I suppose.
To see his reaction. I wish I could promise, Johanna.
I really wish I could. No, that's not true. I'm past the
point of wishing. I never wish, anymore. Do you want
to hear something funny? I hate wishing wells. I do. I
detest them. I find them loathsome. It's true. There's
something I'll bet you didn't know about me. *(Pause)*
I'm not a very good person, Johanna.

JOHANNA: *(Hysterical, screams)* Noooooooooooooo!!!!!!!
(She runs out. Long pause.)

BAL: *(Sincerely, to himself)* I feel very guilty.

Scene Three (b)

(The attic. BAL *and the* CRAP PLAYER *have just finished a game of craps.)*

CRAP PLAYER: *(At the window)* They're still dredging the river for that poor girl.

BAL: *(Counting out money)* Johanna.

CRAP PLAYER: So you did know her.

BAL: Who told you I did? *(No response)* I knew her boyfriend. *(Handing him the money)* Here's eighty, I'll give you the rest on Friday. You don't have to count it.

CRAP PLAYER: *(Counting the money)* My landlady saw her jump. That was fortunate.

BAL: Because she called the police?

CRAP PLAYER: No, because now she has something besides me to talk about. One more game?

*(*BAL *shakes his head, gets a cigarette.)*

CRAP PLAYER: Just want to give you a fair shake. Never know when your luck will turn.

BAL: No such animal as luck.

CRAP PLAYER: No?

BAL: No. If I roll a poor game, there are reasons.

CRAP PLAYER: Are there?

BAL: Reasons because I chose not to shake one more time or one less time. Reasons why I threw hard or not so hard. Reasons for my hands being sweaty—or dry. Reasons. I may be tense. I might be preoccupied. I may be uncomfortable in this shirt—the sleeve might be too tight. Luck's got shit to do with anything. There are reasons.

CRAP PLAYER: If you say so, Bal.

(CRAP PLAYER *starts to leave, stops again at the window. He and* BAL *both look out now. Pause*)

BAL: Women seem more prone to suicide than men. Maybe it has something to do with hormones.

Scene Four (a)

(*River bank. Park bench.* JOHNNY *sits on the bench,* MAN WITH A FISHING POLE *fishes.*)

MAN WITH A FISHING POLE: (*To the fish*) Come on, fishies. Come on now. You're trying my patience. Yum-yum fishies. Yum-yum…. (*Pause. He fishes. Then to* JOHNNY:) I've never seen it like this. Two hours and not a bite. You don't happen to have a match, do you?

(JOHNNY *gives him a match.* MAN *lights it.*)

MAN WITH A FISHING POLE: This is a trick I thought up myself. Burn half of the worm. They like that. Fish are getting more sophisticated every day. Well-done, medium rare. They have their tastes like you or I. Just got to find out what it is, and you got them. (*Fishes*) I give 'em a few more years before they start asking for ketchup and English muffins. Come on now, don't we have any well-done worm lovers in this crowd? (*Pauses; fishes*) Come on fishies. It's chow-time. Soup's on, fishies. I said, soup's on. (*Fishes*) Nothing. Well, I guess I can't blame 'em, I mean I wouldn't bite on no worm, if it is cooked to taste, when I had a whole young girl down there to chew on.

VOICE OFF: They've found her!!!

(MAN WITH A FISHING POLE *quickly collects his things and starts to hurry off.*)

MAN WITH A FISHING POLE: (*To* JOHNNY) You better hurry, fella, if you want to see. They'll be covering her up once they get her on dry ground. (*He runs out.*)

(Pause. JOHNNY *starts to get up, stops. Pause. Suddenly and violently he turns against the bench and begins kicking and hitting it. Boards are broken. He smashes these boards, too, against the bench until finally the bench is a pile of rubble.* JOHNNY *pants. Pause.)*

JOHNNY: *(To himself)* I had to get that out.

Scene Four (b)

(A confessional. Church bells ring. BAL *kneels before a closed curtain. He is sobbing.)*

BAL: *(After a pause)* See, now that's just my point, Father. Do you see? Here I am sobbing. I can't help myself. But the point is not that I can't help myself, but it's the phrase itself—"I am sobbing." Or, rather, it's the idea that I am sobbing, not the phrase. After all, I don't want to make this a linguistic problem. It's the idea that is so terrifyingly inappropriate, or, better, so horrendously untrue. Take my feet, Father. Are *they* sobbing? Can they sob? Or my hair. Or my elbow. What have *they* got to do with sobbing? Have you ever heard the expression— "The sum of all parts"? I am the sum of my parts, Father, so then how can I sob? My eyes, they tear. My throat, it dries. So, then, who or what is doing all this sobbing? *(Short pause)* Not me. It's definitely not me. Each part's too goddamn busy touching the next—like cogs, you see. Like electrical wires. They're much too busy to sob. Oh, I know what you're going to say—I know your argument. You're going to say—if I were to whack a finger off, would that finger still be me? Would that bloody finger over there in the garbage be me? And you'd say, of course it wouldn't. It's not the finger, you'd say, it is the pain. It is what you are feeling which is you. Which is me. But, Father, the pain would only be in here. In here. *(Points to his head)* Just here. Not in my foot. Not in the back of my neck. Only here. So it always comes back to what's in here, does it? *(Pause)* But, Father, I am more than a brain. There's more. There is! I am not just a goddamn brain!!! *(He sobs. Pause. He relaxes.)*

(PRIEST enters from the side, holding a small paper bag.)

PRIEST: Can I help, son?

BAL: *(Standing)* Done. I got it out.

PRIEST: But...?

BAL: I said, I got it out.

(BAL leaves. PRIEST opens the curtain, there is no one there. He takes a cup of coffee out of the bag, opens the lid, sips.)

PRIEST: Next! *(Closes the curtain)*

Scene Five (a)

(BAL's attic. JOHNNY, alone, sits in a chair, waiting. He hears steps and hides. BAL enters with SOPHIE, who is in her twenties.)

SOPHIE: Hey, let go! Let go of my arm!

(BAL lets go.)

SOPHIE: I don't even know who you are. *(Looks around)* Jesus, is this where you live? What are you, a criminal or something? *(Turns back to BAL)* Hey, what makes you think you can just snatch a girl off the street and drag her off to your filthy room?

BAL: You weren't dragged. You walked.

SOPHIE: So I walked. What's that supposed to mean? I was afraid you'd hit me.

BAL: Oh. *(He opens the door so she can leave.)*

SOPHIE: What are you doing? You telling me to leave? What are you, sick? You drag me off the street and up

God knows how many steps to this rat's nest just to tell me to leave? I'll leave when I'm ready to leave. I have to catch my breath.

BAL: Oh. *(He closes the door again.)*

SOPHIE: If I'm not home by nine they'll lock me out.

BAL: There's your incentive to hurry.

SOPHIE: If my mother found out she'd throw me out. My own mother would. I hate her. What's your name?

BAL: Bal.

SOPHIE: That's a stupid name. Mine's Sophie and that's a stupid name too. My grandmother was Sophie too and she was even stupider than her name. What do you do?

BAL: Eat.

SOPHIE: Oh, that's clever. A man who not only lives in a hole in the wall but is clever besides. Boy, this is my lucky day. You want to know what I do?

BAL: No.

SOPHIE: Hey, you've got a great line, you know that? You're a real charmer.

(BAL tries to kiss SOPHIE.)

SOPHIE: Stop that! Haven't you ever heard about conversation? It's when two people talk. One after the other. See, first you talk, then I talk. Or first I talk, then you talk. I'm flexible.

(BAL tries to kiss SOPHIE again.)

SOPHIE: Hold it, will you?

(BAL backs away.)

SOPHIE: Brother, how long you been in this closet, a million years? ...Now, so you want to know what I do, do you, well, I'll tell you....

BAL: *(Screams)* Look!!! *(Calm)* Try for a minute to understand my side of this, okay? I am trying very hard to forget someone. As you may know, there are many ways one can go about accomplishing this. Alcohol is but one. Drugs another. And a third and possibly the best way to forget someone you have had sex with is to find someone else to have sex with. To get that someone else's smell on my body. That sort of thing. I could be more poetic if you want, but I am tired. So that is what I am trying to accomplish, and if it's not going to be you, then I would like to know now while there's still enough time tonight to dig up someone else.

(JOHNNY comes out of hiding. SOPHIE reacts in shock and surprise.)

BAL: Johnny.

(Pause)

JOHNNY: Bal. *(Short pause)* Bal, don't you ever make your bed? Or…change your sheets? I'm not a fanatic or anything, but that's just the kind of thing that would drive me mad. If it were my bed, I mean…. You want me to get some clean sheets? Be no trouble. God, you must have had them on since… for weeks. *(Pause)* It's really a shame about—you know. I mean if I've said it once I've said it a thousand times, someday someone's going to fall into that river. That bank's pretty damn steep…. Not all that steep, but steep. And the current… I've said it a thousand times. *(Pause)* But who knows, you know. A lot of possible things could have happened to…. Anything could have happened. Right? There are a thousand possibilities. *(Pause)* Aren't there?

(Pause)

BAL: Uh. *(Thinks)* No, I don't think so.

(JOHNNY makes a slight groan. Long pause)

BAL: You know, I've been thinking about you. I know at the moment it may not look like it, but I have. I've been thinking a whole lot about you, Johnny. I've been thinking... *(Begins to count out his thoughts)* ...how very sorry I am—not only for Johanna, but also for you. I've been thinking what a jerk you were for letting your girl get to know me. I've been thinking that because you never got the chance yourself, that I've wanted to tell you that Johanna, she was, Johnny, quite a spirited lover. Very lively and instinctual. *(Short pause)* I've been thinking a lot of things, Johnny, but some of those thoughts have been about *you*. *(Pause)* I wanted you to know that. It might help to know that you've been on my mind.

(Pause)

JOHNNY: I'm peeing. *(Short pause. To* SOPHIE.*)* Excuse me, I can't help it. *(His pants are wet.)*

Scene Five (b)

(The attic. BAL *and* SOPHIE *in bed.* JOHNNY *sits at a distance with his head down. In the dark,* BAL *screams.)*

SOPHIE: You scared me half to death.

BAL: *(Turning on a light)* I had a nightmare. *(He sits up.)* Hand me that notepad.

*(*SOPHIE *does and goes back to sleep. To* JOHNNY.*)*

BAL: I have to write down my nightmare before I forget it. *(Writes)* Whenever I have a dream such as I just did, I find I am compelled to get as much as I can down on paper. I take it as almost an obligation. As if my brain were sending signals and clues about me, Bal. *(Writes)* The real trick is to try not to structure the dream. Just get it all down as I remember it. But, of course, some structuring is bound to happen; but that itself can be significant, because what one remembers can tell you as much about yourself as the dream itself can. Maybe more. *(Writes)* There are days when I do nothing but read through years of my dreams. It's after one of those days that I feel that my two feet are firmly planted on the ground. *(Finishes. To* SOPHIE*)* Roll over. Your breath smells.

*(*SOPHIE *rolls over. To* JOHNNY*)*

BAL: What are you doing, Johnny?

JOHNNY: Praying.

BAL: Mankind is so resilient. And that warms my heart. *(Short pause)* But not my feet. *(To* SOPHIE*)* Quit stealing the covers, will you? *(He pulls covers over him and continues to read through his dreams.)*

Scene Six (a)

(A garage. BAL *fiddles with a generator;* JOHNNY *sits and watches;* BOSS *is screaming at an unseen customer.)*

BOSS: So take your lousy generator and shove it!!! You think I care?! You think you're breaking my heart?!! Oh, it's breaking. My heart is breaking. Ouch! Ouch! I said get the hell out of my garage! I don't need any business from an asshole! *(Turns to* BAL *and* JOHNNY*)* Did you hear me? I don't need business from any asshole. Who the hell does that man think I am? What am I, his lackey? Just because he's in a shitty mood, just because he's got a hag for a wife—oh I've seen her. Thank God I was wearing my sunglasses! *(Turns back)* Don't dump on me, fella!! *(Back to* BAL *and* JOHNNY*)* Tell me something, do I look like a shrink? Do I look like I work in a hospital? Then why are so many of my customers mentally sick?!! Tell me that, will you? Will somebody please explain that to me?!! Oh Christ.

(Calms down. Points at BAL*'s generator.)* So what's wrong with that one?

BAL: It's broken.

BOSS: Oh, that's clever, that's very informative. Maybe I should restate my question—what is broken, Mister Bal?

BAL: The casing is cracked. Cracked casing, no vacuum, no vacuum, no pressure, no pressure, no movement, no movement, it's broken.

BOSS: Cute. Very cute. Can you fix it?

(BAL looks over the generator.)

BOSS: I said, can you fix it? Is it fixable?! Watch my lips!

BAL: Have to seal the casing.

BOSS: Good, then do it.

(BAL stands, staring at the BOSS.*)*

BOSS: What are you doing? I said, do it.

(BAL stares.)

BOSS: Oh Christ, I said fix it!

(BAL doesn't move.)

BOSS: Look, I'm not in the mood to take any shit from a punk. I don't need shit from a punk. Do you understand me, punk? *(Pushes him)* Do you, punk? Punk. Punk. Get the hell out of here and don't come back. You make me sick to my stomach. *(Starts to leave, turns to* JOHNNY*)* I don't need any shit from an asshole!

(BOSS leaves. JOHNNY *looks at* BAL. *Pause.* BAL *sits down with the generator. Throughout the beginning of the next speech,* BAL *repairs the generator, sealing the casing with tape, etc.)*

BAL: So I'm fired. I'm out of work. If I'm out of work I'll go on the dole. I'll become part of the idle poor.

My dole will come out of the pockets of the middle
class, who will then grow to resent me. I will have no
incentive to work, because I'll be paid not to work.
I'll wear tennis shoes and carry radios and stand on
streetcorners. Programs will be set up to help me,
which the rest of society will pay for and resent. Then
they will lose *their* incentive. More people on the
dole, less work. Prices will rise. Governments will
get bigger. Maybe I'll get into trouble with the law.
Money will be spent to keep me in jail, then to keep
me out of jail. I will eat other people's money. I will be
an open wound, a gaping hole that devours money....
*(He has fixed the generator. He now turns it on—it works.
He turns it off. Throughout the rest of the speech, he takes
the generator apart, piece by piece.)* On the other hand,
maybe I'm the type who will pull himself up by his
bootstraps. I will forge ahead. Maybe I'll bounce into
a new position and turn this once bad break to my
advantage. Maybe something great and wonderful
will come along and I will learn to feel superior to all
the shmucks I've surpassed. And I will grow to resent
every lazy bugger who has his hand in my pocket or
stuck in my face. And I will learn to project my face
into theirs and refrain: "I did it, why can't they?" And
I will breathe disgust but appear to give handouts
gladly, because gladly I will want to keep them in their
place. While at the same time voting against all social
programs—not out of spite, but as an act of education,
because I will want it shown just whose hand has been
feeding whom.
Or maybe I will become a liberal thinker and drop
phrases like "fairness" and "equal protection" as if I
were a pigeon dropping my shit, while at the same
time I send my kids off to private school and while
at the same time I keep an eye on their Puerto Rican
mammy, making sure she does not get the rickets. Or
the silver.

Or maybe I'll be a good old boy and simply flail
frustrated and angry and call a nigger a nigger, a spade
a spade, and a bottle of beer mother's milk. Or maybe
I'll become a communist. Or a socialist. Or a socialist
with communist leanings, or a social democrat, or a
populist conservative Democrat, or a conservative
populist Democrat with Republican sympathies, or
a Fascist, or a neo-Fascist conservative, or simply a
Fascist communist.
Whatever. There are many possibilities, aren't there?
And we'll just have to wait and see what kind of man
I am. I don't know about you, Johnny, but the future
intrigues me—and I can't wait to watch. *(The generator
is in pieces. He stands, kicks over the generator.)* See, I
know how these things work.

Scene Six (b)

(A road on the way out of town. BAL *and* JOHNNY *sit on the
edge of the road. Evening.* BAL *now has a very large radio,
which is playing very loud dance music. He wears tennis
shoes, which are unlaced.* BAL *is eating a sandwich. He looks
at* JOHNNY, *offers him half of the sandwich,* JOHNNY *shakes
his head.* BAL *turns down the radio.)*

BAL: Eat. Then digest. Then shit. Then fertilize. Then
grow. Then pick. Then eat. We have to eat, Johnny.
We have an obligation to eat. *(Turns up the radio, then
turns it down again)* Johnny, have you ever had that
urge to startle yourself? You know, to do something,
then after you've done it, you're surprised that you
did it. It's not easy, is it? *(Short pause. He belches.)*
Nope, I knew that was coming. *(Pause. Suddenly slaps
himself in the face)* Nah, I wasn't surprised. But I'm
sort of surprised how much that hurt. I wonder if
that counts. No. *(Short pause)* Wait, I have an idea. *(He
stands.)* First I have to think of something else—so

my mind's preoccupied. What should I think about,
Johnny? Wait, I got it. *(Recites)* "Shall I compare thee
to a summer's day...?" *(He suddenly throws his feet out
from under himself and falls.)* No. I caught myself with
my shoulder, so I must have known that was coming.
I'll try it again. *(Stands)* Where was I? *(Recites)* "Shall I
compare thee to a summer's day? Thou art more lovely
and more temperate. Rough winds do... something to
the something buds of May. And something something
something." I can't remember it. That sort of surprises
me. *(He suddenly throws his feet out from under himself
again and falls.)* Nope. The shoulder again. God damn
it. This is difficult, Johnny.

JOHNNY: Bal...?

BAL: *(Getting up)* Johnny, do me a favor, will you, and
divert me for a moment. Come on, divert me. Maybe
if my mind's occupied with something you do, I'll be
able to startle me.

JOHNNY: Bal, I know what you've done.

BAL: So do I. *(Suddenly turns to his side and yells)* There's
Johanna! Look!!!

(JOHNNY looks.)

BAL: God damn it!!! That startled you, but not me.
Well, anyway, thanks for trying. Thanks for trying to
divert me. *(He sits and takes out the sandwich again.)* You
know, I really don't know if maybe I'm just a complete
jerk. I haven't decided yet. *(Pause)* Johnny, have you
ever thought ahead? I mean, have you ever thought
not about what you were doing, but what you were
about to do? And if what you were about to do, you
did, have you ever thought about what you would do
then? And then? Have you ever thought so far ahead
that you forgot that you were breathing? Have you?
I'm asking you, Johnny. I'm very interested in what

other people have to say—it gives me time to catch my breath, before we get back to talking about me.

JOHNNY: Bal...

BAL: *(Interrupting)* On my more confident days, I feel like I am the most fascinating person alive. On my more lethargic days, I am the laziest man there ever was. When I'm thirsty, I'm as parched as a desert. When I piss, it terrifies me to think that there are other toilets flushing clear across the earth.

JOHNNY: Bal, I want to talk.

BAL: I thought we were.

(JOHNNY looks away.)

BAL: Ah! I see. When you say "talk," I'll bet what you really mean is "argue." I understand. What you in fact mean, Johnny, is that you wish me to commit myself to some phrase or some line of thought, so you can cut me off in mid-stride and twist and distort what may have only been meant to be an offhand remark into something I must now defend with my life, for my self-respect. I see.
You want to take the aggressor's role and leave me the defender's. You want to jab away and pick at my words as if they were the last pieces of flesh on a white bone.
And all you'll need is that one phrase out of my mouth and you'll think you've got me pegged and cornered, and me, like a trapped mouse, I'll be too afraid to breathe, too afraid to utter shit, because I'll see you there, set to pounce and criticize and humiliate and abuse, set to make me feel not only less than you—less witty or less eloquent—but also make me feel less a man than I think I am. Fine.
Well, let's try it. Try me. I'm game. Go ahead and answer me. Answer me!!!

JOHNNY: Bal...!

BAL: *(Screaming)* Answer me! Debate! Debate! Debate! *(Suddenly jumping up and down)* I win! I win! I win!

(JOHNNY turns away. BAL shrugs, turns the radio back up.)

BAL: *(Moving to the music)* I'd love to be dancing right now. *(Short pause)* Actually, it's not so much the dancing that I want, as it is the sweating. I'd love to be sweating right now.

Scene Seven (a)

(The edge of the woods. BAL and JOHNNY have stopped walking. SOPHIE is a short distance from them.)

JOHNNY: She must have gone out of her mind trying to find us.

SOPHIE: So?

BAL: She's desperate.

SOPHIE: It wasn't so hard. Really.

JOHNNY: She looks exhausted, doesn't she?

SOPHIE: I'll be all right. Don't worry.

BAL: *(To JOHNNY)* And whenever I see someone who is desperate, I immediately think— "fair game". I wonder why that is.

(Pause)

SOPHIE: You know, you can just tell me to go. You can. *(Pause)* I don't care.... I mean, who cares? *(Silence. To BAL)* My mother locked me out.

JOHNNY: I'm sorry.

SOPHIE: *(To JOHNNY)* Fuck off! *(Pause. To BAL)* She wouldn't even come to the door.... Yeh, and I'm pounding 'til my knuckles start bleeding. And then, see, she sticks her stupid head out the window and starts screaming— "Slut! Slut!"

JOHNNY: Bal...?

SOPHIE: *(Screams)* Leave him alone, he's listening to me!!! *(Pause. She tries to smile but is close to tears. To* BAL.*)* My legs were shaking.

*(*BAL *looks at* SOPHIE.*)*

SOPHIE: I was out there all alone on the street, see, and then like these other heads, you know, they're popping out of other windows. And they're shouting. Some of 'em are even spitting down at me. My mother's yelling to everyone how I hadn't come home that night and how she, you know, didn't have a daughter. It was kind of like being a kid again. Looking up at everybody. You know that feeling? So I start running off and then I fall and cut myself and they're laughing and me, wouldn't you know it, me I'm just trying to be dignified. *(Crying now, but trying not to show it. Pause.)* Bal, I really love you. I do love you, Bal.

BAL: I heard you the first time. *(To* JOHNNY*)* Whenever I hear someone repeating themselves, I immediately think— "desperate."

(Pause)

SOPHIE: *(Very awkward and self-conscious now)* You want me to go, I'll go. I'll understand. I must look a mess. *(Pause)* Look, who's begging? I'm not begging.

(Silence)

JOHNNY: *(Quietly)* How long ago was this?

SOPHIE: *(Shaking)* Do you know what today is?

JOHNNY: *(Shrugs)* Saturday?

SOPHIE: *(Shrugs)* Maybe a week ago. Maybe.

JOHNNY: And since then?

SOPHIE: Bal, I want to be with you!

BAL: If you stay, I'll hurt you. I'll mistreat you. You'll end up despising me.

SOPHIE: I don't believe that.

BAL: *(Yells)* It's true!!! *(Pause. Calmly)* Look, I know me.

Scene Seven (b)

(The woods. Gray. Nearly winter. JOHNNY and SOPHIE stand together watching the sky. BAL, at a distance, stands over what we learn is a corpse. Pause)

JOHNNY: Gray. Going to snow.

SOPHIE: *(Nods)* You can feel it.

JOHNNY: You can. In your bones.

SOPHIE: No. *(Pause)* For me it's the shoulders. I always feel it first in my shoulders. I have sensitive shoulders.

JOHNNY: Huh. For me, it's my bones.

(Pause. They watch the sky.)

SOPHIE: Makes me feel like I'm on a ship.

JOHNNY: What does?

SOPHIE: The snow coming. Like I'm standing on a ship and way over there on the horizon, across the sea, it's coming. And I'm bobbing up and down—watching, leaning on a rail. Of course, I've never been on a ship, but it makes me feel like I'm on one. *(Pause)* It's coming.

(Long pause)

JOHNNY:
"When all aloud the wind doth blow,
And coughing drowns the parson's saw,
And birds sit brooding in the snow,

And Marion's nose looks red and raw;
When roasted crabs hiss in the bowl,
Then nightly sings the staring owl,
`Tu-whit, tu-who!'—
A merry note."

SOPHIE: What's that? Something you made up?

JOHNNY: *(Shakes his head)* Something I know.

(JOHNNY and SOPHIE move toward BAL.)

BAL: *(Over the corpse)* Dust to dust. Rotten flesh to rotten flesh. His eyes are closed. He must have known what was happening to him. Starvation, I would guess.

JOHNNY: *(Retches)* Jesus!

SOPHIE: Bal, can we go?

BAL: Once I asked a doctor what exactly takes place when a body dies. He told me that dead bodies were none of his business. I've been meaning to ask an undertaker ever since. But what I've been able to surmise or what I remember of what I once surmised, from the light reading I had done on the subject, is that more often than not, the heart goes first, then the blood stops flowing, the brain fails once it has used the blood that remained in the brain, then the veins become quickly limp then just as quickly tight, and they stretch and then they crack. The flesh then soaks up what remains of the body's fluids; so the product then is not unlike a marsh, that is where on the surface there are solids, but underneath there is only soft mud.

SOPHIE: Bal, really, it makes me sick.

BAL: That, Sophie, is due totally to your upbringing. Death has been hidden from us, so it frightens us and makes us ill. Actually, a body like this cannot harm you, Sophie. Your fear is all in your head…. Go ahead and touch it.

JOHNNY: Bal!

BAL: Go ahead, Sophie, it won't bite.

SOPHIE: *(Hesitating)* But I...

BAL: Forget it. *(Starts to leave)*

SOPHIE: No, Bal, wait! *(She touches it.)* It's spongy.

JOHNNY: Why do you listen to him?

BAL: See, it didn't jump up and eat you.... Now kiss it. Come on, on the mouth.

JOHNNY: Bal, how can you ask her to do that?

(BAL shrugs.)

SOPHIE: Kiss it? Oh, I can't, Bal. Really I...

BAL: *(Moves to leave)* Suit yourself.

SOPHIE: Wait, Bal!

(BAL stops. She bends down and kisses the corpse.)

SOPHIE: Worms!

(SOPHIE chokes. Pause. They start to leave.)

JOHNNY: Bal, aren't you going to touch it?

BAL: Me? *(Pause)* No. No, corpses give me the willies.

Scene Seven (c)

(A hut. BAL and JOHNNY sit at a table drinking. SOPHIE sits on a bed, sobbing. She is slowly taking off her clothes, getting ready for bed. Pause.)

BAL: *(To JOHNNY)* Excuse me. *(He walks over to SOPHIE.)* You're crying. You're upset. You're feeling terrible. Eyes bloodshot. Hands pale. You're trembling. You have regrets. Regret after regret. You have a tear that has crawled all the way to your chin. *(He moves away, turns back.)* It helps to know how you are. *(Returns to the table)*

(SOPHIE *continues to sob, though very quietly now. Long pause)*

JOHNNY: Why don't I leave? Was that the question?

BAL: Yes.

(Silence)

JOHNNY: The way you abuse that woman makes me sick to my stomach.

BAL: Is that just a way of speaking, or is your reaction really so physical?

(JOHNNY *looks away.)*

BAL: Just curious. *(Silence)* Johanna.

(JOHNNY *looks back at* BAL.)*

BAL: Did I say something wrong? Can I help it if when I look at you I think of her? If I see your eyes and remember hers? That's how my mind works. Can I help that? *(He puts his head on the table and cries.)* The problem with tears is that they are difficult to read. Even from the inside. Once I thought I was very sad, but I only had a speck of dust on my pupil. I've had a similar experience with a lump in my throat. Whenever I now feel a lump in my throat, I immediately think— "chicken bone." *(Pours drinks for himself and* JOHNNY.)*

(Silence)

JOHNNY: *(A little drunk)* What you said about the lump in your throat and the chicken bone made me think about a certain park bench. I shattered this bench with my own hands. When I was through I felt a lot better. I felt better because my hand hurt now. The pain was there. I could see it. *(Suddenly, he takes out a notepad and writes furiously; finishes.)*

BAL: *(Takes what* JOHNNY *has just written and reads)* "Sunday in January. Bal cries. He talks of sadness. All I want to do is slit his throat. I want to take a broken bottle—a green broken bottle, or a red one with two jagged edges, and I want to hold it right next to his throat and I want to watch his eyes. I want that. I want to slit that throat. The throat. His..." *(To* JOHNNY*)* What's this word?

JOHNNY: *(Looks at the notepad)* "Throat."

BAL: "His throat. His throat. Please." *(Pause. He hands back the notepad.)* It helps to get upset every once in a while.

*(*SOPHIE *cries.* JOHNNY *is almost frozen.* BAL *stands, looks at one and then the other, and puts out one hand for each of them.)*

BAL: *(Proud)* We're a very emotional group. We are. *(Smiles)*

Scene Seven (d)

(The hut. BAL *and* JOHNNY *at the table, as before.* SOPHIE *is asleep in bed. Pause.* JOHNNY *stands and begins to strip down to his shorts. He sits back down.)*

JOHNNY: Hot.

*(*BAL *nods. Pause.)*

BAL: *(Points to the bed)* You want to get in?

JOHNNY: What are you, a pimp?

BAL: You don't want to fuck her?

JOHNNY: You're disgusting. She's in love with you.

BAL: Her mother wouldn't let her back in, she had nowhere to go, she felt like the world had closed in on her, she'd run out of options, she ran into us, "an option," she told herself, so she fell in love.

JOHNNY: Is that what you think?

BAL: That's what I think, whether it's true or not. But it is what I think and that is what matters, doesn't it?

(Pause. BAL *goes to the bed, picks up the covers and shows* SOPHIE, *who is naked, to* JOHNNY.*)*

JOHNNY: Bal, what do you want?

BAL: I want to entice you into bed with her. I've got it into my head that the sight of you two in a good healthy clinch would be pleasing to me. Though at the same time, I am feeling rather guilty at the thought. I'm wondering—is that a sick thought? Does this show me up as having certain perverse inclinations? And then I'm thinking—but it's society that dictates what is and is not perverse. And then I'm thinking—but I am part of society. And then I'm thinking—I am what I am.

JOHNNY: Go to hell.

*(*JOHNNY *turns away.* BAL *shrugs and goes back to the table. Pause)*

BAL: Isn't there anything I can do for you? Something? There must be. You just have to let me know, Johnny. You just have to let me help. I want to offer my help.

JOHNNY: Why?

BAL: I enjoy the feeling.

JOHNNY: Ah.

(Short pause)

BAL: Once I saw a child screaming in the street. He came up to me and asked me to take him home, to his mother. I said, sure, kid. I said—sure.

JOHNNY: And?

BAL: And then I left him. I felt terrific. What more could I do? I offered. Isn't that enough? I'm offering, Johnny, isn't that enough?

(SOPHIE *wakes up, gets out of bed—naked.*)

SOPHIE: I'm going to get myself a beer. Anyone want one?

(BAL *and* JOHNNY *don't respond;* SOPHIE *shrugs and exits.*)

BAL: (*To* JOHNNY) Hot?

Scene Seven (e)

(*The hut. Night.* JOHNNY *and* SOPHIE *in bed, asleep in each other's arms.* BAL *enters. He suddenly rips the covers off them. They shriek.*)

BAL: Peek-a-boo!

(BAL *laughs and giggles with childish pleasure.* SOPHIE *and* JOHNNY *just stare at him.*)

SOPHIE: (*Coldly, to* JOHNNY) He's drunk.

(JOHNNY *and* SOPHIE *cover themselves up. Pause*)

BAL: (*Quietly*) Yes. (*Short pause*) Everything is chemical.

Scene Seven (f)

(*A clearing near a pond.* JOHNNY *and* SOPHIE *have just run in, out of breath, though smiling. They have been swimming and are naked.* BAL *sits at a distance.*)

JOHNNY: (*Toweling himself*) One more dip?

SOPHIE: Hand me my blouse.

JOHNNY: It's not cold. It's rather refreshing. I feel refreshed.

(SOPHIE *takes her blouse.*)

JOHNNY: Don't you?

(SOPHIE *giggles.*)

JOHNNY: No?

(SOPHIE *giggles again.*)

JOHNNY: Might be the last pond for days.

SOPHIE: Might.

JOHNNY: Best make the best of it. You look refreshed.

(SOPHIE *giggles again*)

JOHNNY: You do. I'll go myself then. (*Smiling, he slaps her fanny with the towel.*) I will. (*He does it again.*)

SOPHIE: (*Laughing, slaps him back—all very playful*) No you won't. Nope.

JOHNNY: (*Continuing*) Here I go! I'm going!

(JOHNNY *and* SOPHIE *stop and just stand and laugh. She suddenly becomes quiet.*)

SOPHIE: (*With a faint smile*) One more dip. (*She begins to take her blouse off.*)

BAL: (*Calmly*) You two are disgusting.

(JOHNNY *and* SOPHIE *stop and turn to him.*)

BAL: You are. They way you act. You take off your clothes right in front of me. Paw each other. Prance around. You're shameless. You're disgusting.... I don't mean that as a criticism. I'm not saying that's either good or bad. All I'm saying is that that is what is generally meant by the word "disgusting". Isn't it?

(*Slowly they begin to put their clothes on.*)

BAL: I mean, you two fit the definition. I'm not saying this against you. I don't mean that. Don't misunderstand me.... What's wrong? What did I do?

(JOHNNY *and* SOPHIE *are very somber.*)

BAL: Hey, doesn't anyone want to talk ideas anymore???

Scene Eight (a)

(Plain. Wind. BAL *enters. He holds his hair back and sticks his face into the wind.)*

BAL: Ahhh. Listen to that wind. *(Makes wind noise)* Mmmmmmm. Feel it. Ahhh. *(Makes wind noise. Softly.)* Blow. Blow. Blow. Yes. Ahhhhh. *(Laughs with great pleasure)*

(JOHNNY *enters. He is cold.)*

JOHNNY: *(Shivering)* Shit.

BAL: Have we lost her?

JOHNNY: You'd like that, wouldn't you?

BAL: I don't know what I'd like. At the moment my mind's pretty much blank. If anything, I guess you could say I'm concentrating on walking, though there is a little tune that keeps running through my mind. *(Starts to leave, stops; to* JOHNNY) Do you hear it? *(He exits.)*

JOHNNY: *(Calls)* Sophie! Sophie!

(JOHNNY *runs out. Pause. He reenters with* SOPHIE, *who is pregnant now.)*

SOPHIE: *(Entering)* That's a hard question for me to answer, Johnny. I'm not sure why I won't go off with you. You'd make a hell of a better father than Bal ever would. You'd be reliable. I could trust you. But I just have this fixed idea in my head that Bal is the man for me. And I can't let go of the thought. I just can't help myself. *(She starts to leave.)*

JOHNNY: *(Quietly)* Sophie?

(She stops; they stare at each other.)

SOPHIE: Johnny, *you* see someone in trouble and you just have to help. You're one of those kind. You are. *(She turns to leave.)*

JOHNNY: Sophie!!

(SOPHIE stops.)

JOHNNY: Sophie, I just want you to know—Jesus Christ, I can't believe I'm going to say this—

SOPHIE: Say what, Johnny?

JOHNNY: If it matters so much to you, Sophie, I just want to tell you that I can be pretty damn cruel myself. I can be disgusting. I could abuse you. Whatever you want.

SOPHIE: Oh. *(Pause)* What do you know. I was wrong about you. You're not one of those good people like I thought you were, Johnny. You're one of those who will do whatever they can to get what they want. An opportunist. I understand. Oh that's what you are.

(SOPHIE turns to leave, sees BAL, who has reentered. She turns back to JOHNNY.)

SOPHIE: Johnny, I just remembered, Bal has asked me to ask you something.

(JOHNNY nods, waits to be told.)

SOPHIE: He wants you to start calling me Johanna. I have no idea why.

(SOPHIE leaves. JOHNNY turns to BAL. Silence)

BAL: *(Shrugs; quietly)* You know me, Johnny—I can't help myself.

Scene Eight (b)

(A field. JOHNNY *and* SOPHIE *with the* BABY. BAL, *at a great distance, lies on his back, staring at the sky.)*

JOHNNY: *(To* BABY*)* Goo. Goo. Goo-goo. Cute.

SOPHIE: It's not crying. When it's not crying, I start to worry. I start waiting for it to cry. Then I try to shut it up. Then it shuts up and I worry.... It needs me.

JOHNNY: *(Playing with the* BABY*)* Tell me something, do you think I'm the type of person who would kill himself? Am I that type of person? *(Smiles at the* BABY*)* Am I?

SOPHIE: I wouldn't know.

JOHNNY: *(Without looking up)* But you do know. You know all about suicide.

SOPHIE: Do I? Mmmmmm. *(Picks up the* BABY*)* If I were to let it go, it would die. What a strange thought.

JOHNNY: *(Watching the* BABY*)* Well, I think I am the type. That's what I think. Gaga. Goo-goo. Pinky toes.... How do you think you'd react to my death, Johanna?

SOPHIE: Mmmmmm.

JOHNNY: *(To* BABY*)* Boo.

SOPHIE: I guess I'd be sad. Though my sadness would soon pass. Then I'd worry that my sadness passed too quickly, because I was brought up to feel sad for a long time. Or maybe I was brought up to feel bad that my sadness passes too quickly.

JOHNNY: Maybe. It's watching me.

SOPHIE: Yes.

JOHNNY: *(Playing with the* BABY*)* I love you, Johanna.

SOPHIE: I doubt it.

JOHNNY: *(Thinking seriously about it)* Maybe you're right, now that you mention it. Maybe I just want to take you away from him. Maybe all I'm really thinking is "beat him" and you're just the stakes. Maybe I'm thinking all I want is to see his face when you go away with me. I don't know. But that's what I'm thinking. And then I'm thinking—is that so bad? I'm thinking is that abnormal?

SOPHIE: You know who you sound like?

JOHNNY: Who? I'm always interested in how other people see me.

(The BABY *makes a noise.)*

SOPHIE: Goo. Goo. *(Cradling the* BABY*)* No doubt I'll slap it silly when it gets old enough to answer back.

JOHNNY: No doubt, Johanna. Goo. Goo.

Scene Eight (c)

(A plain. Cold. BAL, JOHNNY, *and* SOPHIE, *who carries the* BABY *in a sling across her front, enter.)*

BAL: It's getting dark, let's camp here.

JOHNNY: Bal, there's a village just up the way. Look, you can see the lights.

BAL: So?

JOHNNY: There'll be decent food in that village. And beds. Warm beds.

BAL: So?

JOHNNY: So then how can you make them sleep in the dirt another night when all we have to do is walk another ten, maybe fifteen minutes to make them and ourselves comfortable?

SOPHIE: Bal, we really wouldn't mind a bed now. And a bath. We'd kill for a hot bath.

BAL: Uh-huh.

JOHNNY: Then it's settled, let's go before it gets any darker.

BAL: No. I don't want to.

JOHNNY: For Christ's sake, why?

BAL: *(Quietly)* Two men and a woman with a baby. It'd look funny. People would talk. They'd stare. Innuendos would be made. I'd feel embarrassed. I might blush. I try to avoid situations like that.

JOHNNY: And that's your reason?

(BAL nods.)

JOHNNY: And what about her?

(BAL shrugs.)

JOHNNY: And the baby?

BAL: Okay, you've succeeded.

JOHNNY: Then we'll go into the village?

BAL: No. You succeeded in getting me to dislike myself.

(BAL rubs his hands together, blows on them. JOHNNY turns away.)

BAL: Cold.

(BAL stops rubbing, looks at SOPHIE, walks up behind her, puts his arms around her and hugs. She presses her head against his shoulder.)

BAL: Warm.

(JOHNNY turns back, he is crying now. BAL looks at him, lets go of SOPHIE, and moves to JOHNNY, almost runs to him with arms outstretched and hugs him. JOHNNY cries on his shoulder.)

BAL: Warm.

(SOPHIE *joins them and snuggles against them. The three hug.* BAL *moves away, feels his hands.*)

BAL: Better. *(He takes out a bottle, starts to drink, stops.)* Don't even bother to ask, there's only enough booze left for me.

(JOHNNY *and* SOPHIE *nod,* BAL *drinks.*)

JOHNNY: *(Touching his tears)* It's raining.

SOPHIE: *(Hugs the baby)* Warm.

BAL: *(Finishing the booze)* Better.

Scene Nine

(A tree. JOHNNY, *alone, sits on the ground with a long piece of rope. Throughout the beginning of the speech, he ties the rope into a noose.)*

JOHNNY: *(To the audience)* Honestly, I never dreamed I would find myself in a situation like this, and even if I had *imagined* the possibility, no doubt I would have imagined the experience of the situation to be quite different. I would have thought my head would be filled with images of my life. That is—I would have thought I'd be "seeing my life pass before me." Or another possibility—I would have thought I'd find some humor in my situation. I've read about certain individuals who have survived such experiences as this and who claim at the very last moment they found themselves funny. And they laughed. I can understand that. *(He finishes the knot, tries it on, takes it off, looks up at the tree.)* Or yet a third imaginable possibility would have been to be consumed by thoughts of my own funeral. Who would come? What would they say? Will I be missed? So—if someone would have come up to me a year or so ago and asked me what I would

be thinking at the moment of my death, I no doubt
would have said one of *these* possibilities—or perhaps
some grouping of these possibilities. And I would
have felt quite confident that I was correct. (*He throws
the rope over the branch of the tree.*) However, I know
now—from experience—how wrong I really would
have been. Because my one urge now, in fact my only
urge—is to talk. (*He puts the noose around his neck, climbs
up on a stump.*) It's as if my mouth was the only chunk
of me that is not yet ready to be nailed shut. It's like
I'm just not talked out yet. So here—at the point of
suicide—I find that my greatest concern is in finding
something interesting to say. (*Pause. He tests the rope.*)
So—what do I end up saying? What have I found to
talk about? *Possibilities*—that's what. The possibility
of imagining my life pass before me. The possibility of
finding humor in my death. Possibilities. (*Pause*) You
know, Johanna was wrong. She said I was one of those
who will do whatever they can to get what they want.
That's not me. I'm no opportunist. A man who thinks
only about possibilities at the moment of his death is
but one thing—an optimist. And that's just what I am. I
am a hopeless optimist. That's me alright.

(JOHNNY *jumps. Blackout. Suddenly we hear a* FEMALE
SINGER *singing a sad song.*)

Scene Ten

(*A nightclub. In the black we hear the final refrain of the sad
song, then wild applause.* BAL *and* CRONY *sit at a table.*
CRONY *reads a newspaper.* FEMALE SINGER *stands next to*
BAL. WAITER *stands at a distance.*)

FEMALE SINGER: I'm told you want to buy me a drink.

BAL: I do.

FEMALE SINGER: *(Sitting)* I haven't seen you around here before.

BAL: No.

(CRONY turns a page.)

FEMALE SINGER: Well, did you enjoy the show?

BAL: *(Perking up)* Your first song moved me. I was all yours. I followed every lyric.

FEMALE SINGER: *(Relaxes)* How wonderful.

BAL: *(Smiles)* Then with the second my mind began to wander. It did. I began to watch your throat. I began to watch how you breathed.

FEMALE SINGER: *(Uncomfortable)* Uh-huh.

BAL: Yes. And then I watched the lights. Then the people at other tables. By the third song I was lost in my own thoughts. I wondered whether I should leave. I wanted to be somewhere else.

FEMALE SINGER: What?!

BAL: *(Continuing)* I played with my ice.

FEMALE SINGER: You…?

BAL: …played with my ice. By the fourth song I'd forgotten you. You were like traffic in the background.

FEMALE SINGER: *(Standing up, to WAITER)* Is this somebody's idea of a joke?!! *(She leaves.)*

BAL: *(Calling after her)* By the fifth song, you were a slight irritation. Like something in my eye. Like a pebble in my boot! *(He shrugs. Drinks)*

CRONY: *(Pointing to a picture in the paper)* Did you catch this? Poor boy—found hanging in the forest.

BAL: *(Looks. He is surprised.)* Johnny.

CRONY: You knew him?

BAL: I knew his girlfriend. *(Short pause)* So that's the kind of person he was.

CRONY: What kind of person is that?

BAL: The kind who can only take so much. *(Short pause)* I feel terrible. He shouldn't have killed himself. I wouldn't feel like this if he hadn't. *(Pause. He shakes his head, obviously upset. Then he suddenly notices his position.)* I remember seeing a movie once where a man sat in just such a position as this, holding just such a glass out in front of him. He talked to himself too. *(Pause)* Ever since then, this position has become for me—the drowning-one's-sorrows position. *(Breaks the position, nods)* We never stop learning how to behave. *(Works himself back into the "drowning-one's sorrows-position".)*

END OF PLAY